HOW THINGS HAVE CHANGED

Toys

JON RICHARDS

Chrysalis Children's Books

501276118

First published in the UK in 2004 by
Chrysalis Children's Books
An imprint of Chrysalis Books Group Plc
The Chrysalis Building, Bramley Road,
London W10 6SP

ISBN 1 84458 112 8

British Library Cataloguing in Publication Data for this
book is available from the British Library.

Editorial Manager *Joyce Bentley*
Editorial Assistant *Camilla Lloyd*
Produced by Tall Tree Ltd
Designer Ed Simkins
Editor *Kate Simkins*
Consultant *Jon Kirkwood*
Picture Researcher *Lorna Ainger*

Printed in China

Some of the more unfamiliar words used in this book
are explained in the glossary on page 31.

Typography *Natascha Frensch*
Read Regular, READ SMALLCAPS and Read Space;
European Community Design Registration 2003 and
Copyright © Natascha Frensch 2001-2004
Read Medium, Read Black and *Read Slanted*
Copyright © Natascha Frensch 2003-2004

READ™ is a revolutionary new typeface that will enchance
children's understanding through clear, easily recognisable
character shapes. With its evenly spaced and carefully
designed characters, READ™ will help children at all stages
to improve their literacy skills, and is ideal for young readers,
reluctant readers and especially children with dyslexia.

Photo Credits:
The publishers would like to thank the following for their kind permission to
reproduce the photographs:

Lorna Ainger: FCtl, 5t, 17b, 27b, 29tc, 29tr Alamy: Tony Cordoza FCc, 27t,
Paul Whitehill 19b Corbis: Christie's Images 12 Getty Images: 24, AFP 14, 28bl,
AFP/Damien Meyer 21b, Hulton Archive 9tr, 20, Mario Tama 15b, Time Life/Alfred
Eisenstadt 24, Time Life/Ralph Morse FCbr, 11b Robert Opie: FCbl, BC, 1, 4, 5b, 6,
7, 8, 9bl, 10, 16, 17t, 18, 19t, 21t, 22, 23, 25, 28br, 29bl, 30, 31 Rex Features
Ltd.: 26 Tall Tree Ltd.: 2, 13, 15t, 28tr Courtesy Wrebbit: FCtr, 11t

Contents

Little people

Dolls are toys based on human figures and are some of the oldest known toys. Today's dolls can have movable joints, voices and the latest fashion accessories.

Wooden dolls from around 3000 BC have been found in Ancient Egyptian graves, but there were probably even earlier dolls that have not survived. By the 15th century, doll makers in Germany were earning a living producing these toys.

◄ The earliest known doll's house was made in 1558 for Duke Albrecht V of Bavaria. This one dates from around 1875.

Early dolls were based on adult figures, but during the 19th century, dolls of babies became very popular. Today's dolls range from crying babies that need nappy changing to stylish models with the latest designer outfits. There are even dolls that look like pop stars, such as Britney Spears.

◄ Over a billion Barbie dolls have been sold around the world since it was first released in 1959, making it the world's most popular doll.

LOOK CLOSER

The GI Joe action figure was released in the US in 1964 and was the first doll for boys. It was introduced to the UK two years later under the name Action Man. Over 250 million of these figures have been sold around the world.

Cute and cuddly

Soft toys have long been a favourite toy for children to hold and cuddle. The earliest soft toys were simple rag dolls, but today they can be computer-controlled, brightly coloured characters.

Very little is known about the history of soft toys as few have lasted – their soft materials tend to rot. One of the oldest surviving examples is a rag doll dating from Ancient Rome between 300 and 200 BC.

◄ This rabbit toy from about 1900 is stuffed with wood wool – fine shavings of wood.

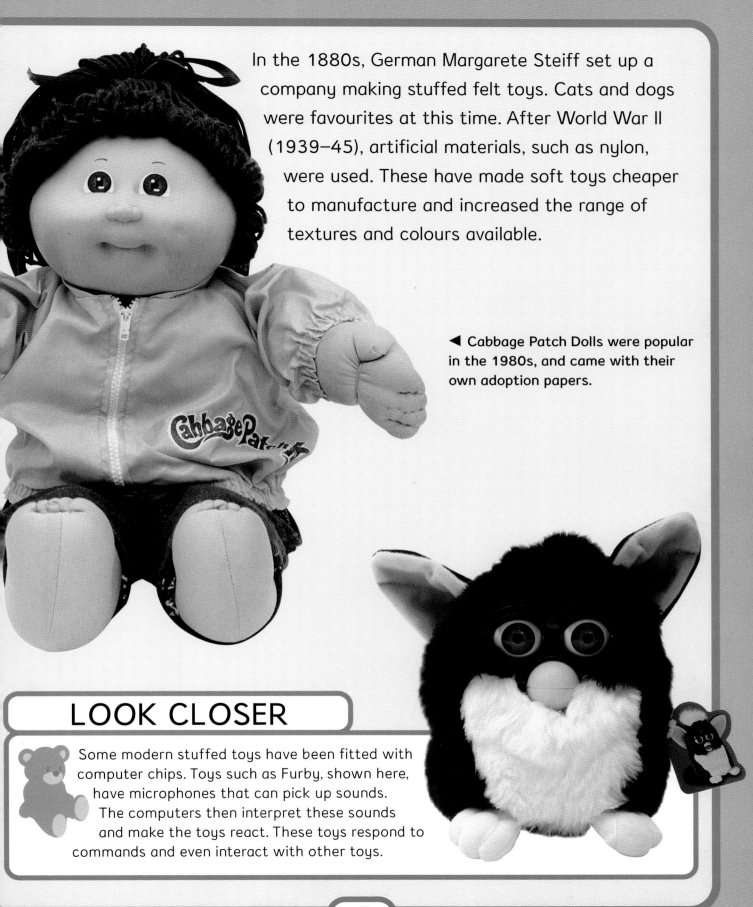

In the 1880s, German Margarete Steiff set up a company making stuffed felt toys. Cats and dogs were favourites at this time. After World War II (1939–45), artificial materials, such as nylon, were used. These have made soft toys cheaper to manufacture and increased the range of textures and colours available.

◀ Cabbage Patch Dolls were popular in the 1980s, and came with their own adoption papers.

LOOK CLOSER

Some modern stuffed toys have been fitted with computer chips. Toys such as Furby, shown here, have microphones that can pick up sounds. The computers then interpret these sounds and make the toys react. These toys respond to commands and even interact with other toys.

Teddy bears

Since they were introduced in the 1900s, teddy bears have become a favourite companion for children at bedtime. They owe their name to a president of the USA.

The Steiff company from Germany made its first stuffed bear in 1902. Steiff bears remain popular today and can be recognised by the button sewn into one of the bear's ears.

◄ Like modern bears, this old Steiff bear has movable limbs. Today, these antique bears are valuable collector's items.

EUREKA!

It is said that in 1902, the president of the USA, Theodore 'Teddy' Roosevelt (right), was hunting when he refused to shoot a bear cub. On seeing a cartoon showing this event, Morris Michtom started to produce stuffed toy bears, calling them 'teddy bears' after the president.

Care Bears
Les Bisounours / Troetel-beertjes

Good Luck Bear™

Teddy bears have changed very little since they first appeared, although most are now made of artificial materials. Other innovations include a growl or a voice. There are even teddy bears that can be heated in a microwave oven and taken to bed warm!

◄ Care Bears were first sold in the 1980s. Between 1983 and 1987, over 40 million of these bears were sold, due to the popularity of their movies and TV shows.

Brain teasers

Puzzles are one of the few toys that are designed for both adults and children. They range from jigsaws to maths or word puzzles. They are ideal learning toys as they encourage people to solve problems while they play.

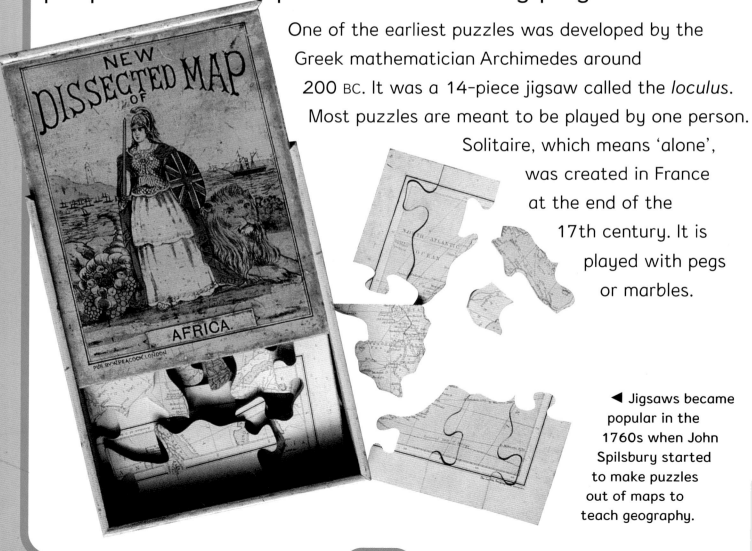

One of the earliest puzzles was developed by the Greek mathematician Archimedes around 200 BC. It was a 14-piece jigsaw called the *loculus*. Most puzzles are meant to be played by one person. Solitaire, which means 'alone', was created in France at the end of the 17th century. It is played with pegs or marbles.

◀ Jigsaws became popular in the 1760s when John Spilsbury started to make puzzles out of maps to teach geography.

One of the most popular puzzles are crosswords, which were introduced in 1913. These can be found in books, newspapers and magazines. Three-dimensional puzzles are based on the jigsaw. They are made of thick cardboard to make the structure rigid.

◄ Some modern jigsaw puzzles come in three dimensions, allowing people to recreate famous buildings.

EUREKA!

In the 1970s, Hungarian architect Erno Rubik developed a cube puzzle to help his students learn how to solve problems. It was marketed globally in 1980 and went on to be an enormous success, with over 100 million Rubik's cubes sold.

The full deck

Hundreds of card games, such as bridge and poker, are played with the traditional deck of cards. More recent games use new types of cards, such as collecting cards and trump sets.

The earliest reference to playing cards comes from China around AD 950. Their use had spread to Europe via the Middle East by the 14th century.

▼ This scene shows a group of people playing cards in the 18th century. Many card games that are still played today, such as whist, were developed at this time.

EUREKA!

The suits of a traditional deck of cards are French in origin and date from about 1470. These original suits were: *carreau* ('square'), which became diamonds in English; *trèfle* ('three leaves'), which became clubs; *pique* ('pike'), which became spades; and *coeur* ('heart'), which remained hearts.

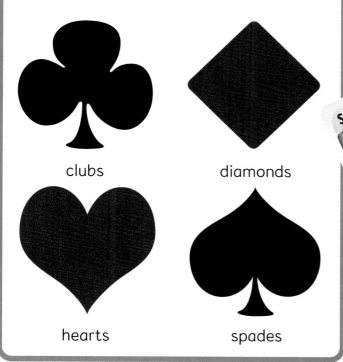

clubs

diamonds

hearts

spades

Cards proved popular because they were cheap to make and new games could be created easily. These included primero, an early version of poker that was developed in the 16th century, and gin rummy, which was first played in 1909. Newer types of card games include happy families and battling cards, such as Pokémon.

▲ These Pokémon cards were created in 1996 and contain statistics about each character. They are collected and swapped.

Board games

The first board games were created over 9000 years ago. Some of the earliest, such as chess, were based on battlefield tactics. More recent games have been inspired by all sorts of things, from crosswords to films and television.

Early board games that were based on battle tactics used different pieces to represent military units, such as infantry, chariots, elephants and cavalry. One example, called *chaturanga*, appeared in India around AD 600 and was the forerunner of chess.

◀ Backgammon has origins that date back to **3000** BC.

Snakes and ladders, which dates back to the 12th century, was designed to show children the benefits of good behaviour. More recent board games reflect modern interests, such as property ownership in Monopoly (created 1933) and general knowledge in Trivial Pursuit (created 1979).

▲ Hundreds of different versions of Monopoly have been created using street names from cities around the world and even film and TV characters.

EUREKA!

The design and look of chess has changed greatly since it first appeared. A two-coloured board was introduced around AD 1000, and the queen piece had more power after 1475. The designs for the pieces used in today's standard chess set were established in 1835.

Toy figures

Toy figures are small copies of people, animals and characters. They have been used by children and collectors to re-create scenes, from a small farmyard to a full-scale battle.

One of the oldest surviving toy figures is a 4000-year-old model of oxen pulling a cart from the Indus Valley civilisation. Early figures were made from natural materials. They were flat and cut out from a sheet of wood or metal.

▼ These cavalry soldiers from the late 1890s were manufactured by Britains, the first company to produce fully rounded figures.

Fully rounded toy figures were introduced in 1893 when companies started to use industrial moulding to make toys. Today, modern materials, such as plastic, mean that toy figures are cheaper and easier to make, allowing manufacturers to produce them in large quantities.

◄ Many of today's action figures are based on characters from movies, such as this Chewbacca figure from the Star Wars films.

LOOK CLOSER

Since the 1930s, toy manufacturers have used film and, later, TV characters to sell toys. They buy a licence to make these toys from the people who created the characters. Today, nearly every movie released comes with its own toys, such as the Harry Potter and Disney toys shown here.

Construction toys

Building and modelling toys have been around for more than two hundred years. These popular playthings encourage children to use their imagination and be creative.

The first construction sets were introduced at the end of the 18th century. They consisted of simple shapes, many of which were printed with letters and numbers on them for adding and spelling games.

▼ This building set from 1900 is made up of shapes that can be stacked on top of each other to create buildings.

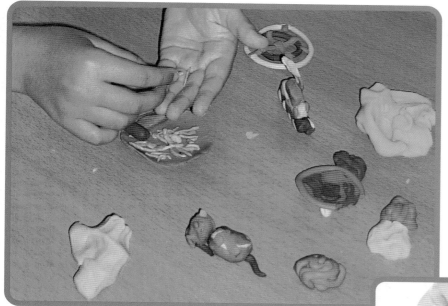

British art teacher William Harbutt developed Plasticine, a modelling clay that never sets, in 1897 when his students complained that the clay they were using dried too quickly.

By the 20th century, new materials were being used to make building sets. In 1901, Frank Hornby developed Meccano, a system of metal strips that were bolted together. Other materials included clay and plastic, which are more flexible.

EUREKA!

In 1958, Danish toy manufacturer Ole Kirk Christiansen and his LEGO company patented a design of plastic building bricks with studs and holes to allow them to stick together. The bricks became very popular and, today, LEGO is sold around the world.

Activity toys

Some toys are designed to be part of an active pastime, offering exercise as well as something that's fun to play with. These activity toys range from simple bats and balls to the latest skateboards and in-line skates.

Ancient activity toys include hoops that were depicted in Ancient Egyptian tomb paintings dating from 2500 BC. Yo-yos were also popular toys in Ancient Greece and China.

▼ Kites were flown in China over 3000 years ago. These were made of silk and bamboo and were often shaped like animals.

The first roller skates were developed in the 1760s by Belgian Joseph Merlin. In 1980, ice hockey player Scott Olsen designed modern in-line skates, which had the wheels in a single row for greater stability. In 1958, Bill Richards fitted wheels to a strip of wood to create the first skateboard.

▲ Hoops have been a popular toy for thousands of years, often pushed along with a stick. In 1958, the hula hoop, which was spun around the waist, was launched and became a huge success.

EUREKA!

In 1871, William Russell Frisbie founded a pie factory near Yale College. His pies became popular with students, who then used the pie containers as a toy, throwing them to one another. In 1948, Fred Morrison produced plastic discs and called them Frisbees, misspelling the pie maker's name.

Wind them up

Toys that power themselves have been around for nearly 2500 years. They were driven by steam, water, compressed air and coiled springs. These powered devices include musical boxes, moving cars, train sets and walking robots.

One of the first references to a mechanical toy mentions an Ancient Greek called Archytas who built a mechanical bird around 400 BC. Nearly 2000 years later, the invention of the coiled spring in the 15th century led to the creation of clockwork motors.

◀ Early musical boxes, such as this Symphonion, were powered by clockwork.

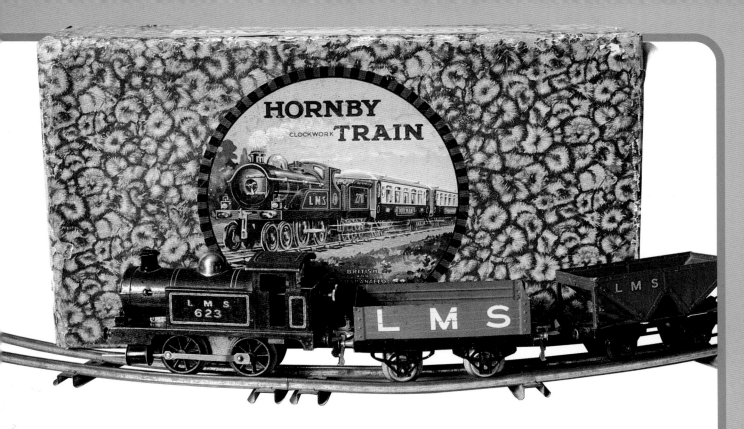

At first, clockwork motors were used only in clocks and watches, but in the 19th century, they were fitted to miniature trains to create the first clockwork toys. Clockwork motors remained popular in toys for many years, before they were replaced by electric motors from the middle of the 20th century.

▲ The earliest clockwork trains would simply run on the floor. Later models, such as this one from the 1930s, came with their own tracks.

LOOK CLOSER

Robot toys first appeared just after World War II. Leading the way were a number of Japanese companies that were successful with a robot toy based on the character Robby the Robot from the 1956 film *Forbidden Planet*. Since then, plastic has replaced tin, making robot toys cheaper and easier to make. Today's robot toys, such as the Transformers, have their own TV shows.

Electric toys

Electric toys are fitted with small motors that are powered by an electric current from the mains or batteries.

The earliest electrical motors were fitted to toys, such as train sets, in the 1890s. These new toys could be played with for hours without the need to wind them up or refuel them.

▼ This train set from the 1950s is powered by electricity supplied along cables plugged into the mains supply.

By the 1950s, most homes had mains electricity and small electric motors became more powerful and easier to manufacture. The result was a surge in the popularity of electric toys, including slot car sets and talking dolls. The development of small electrical batteries allowed manufacturers to produce portable powered toys.

▲ Slot car racing, such as Scalextric, gets its name from the metal slot cut into the track from which the cars pick up their power. Scalextric toys were first produced in 1958. Today's sets include the Formula One, GT40 Sport, Le Mans 24-Hour and the Touring Challenge versions.

LOOK CLOSER

Radio-controlled vehicles can be steered from a distance without using wires. The hand-held controller sends commands to an electric device in the vehicle, telling it how to move.

Computer games

Computer games started as a way of illustrating how far early computers had advanced. As computers became more powerful, so the games became more complex and varied.

The earliest computer games, such as Spacewar! from 1962, were only available to computer programmers. The 1970s saw the introduction of the first arcade games, home computers and games consoles. Their popularity made games such as Pacman and Space Invaders household names.

◀ Space Invaders was one of the first video games to appear in arcades. It was introduced in 1978.

The Internet has created another boom in the games industry. People can now play fast-action games with someone in another country. Games and consoles, such as Playstation 2 and Xbox, are now fitted with Internet capability as standard.

Computers have become more powerful, allowing programmers to make games more and more realistic. Today, there are hand-held consoles, mobile phones with computer games and games you can play on the Internet.

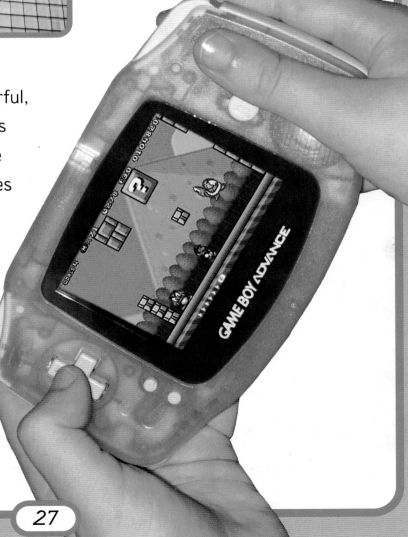

▶ When it was released in 1989, the Game Boy was an instant success and is still popular today. New games can be bought or swapped and simply slotted into the machine.

Timeline

- C.AD 600. A forerunner of chess called *chaturanga* is developed in India.

- C.1100. Snakes and ladders is developed.

- C.1470. The modern suits in a deck of cards are introduced in France.

- 1558. The earlies[t] known doll's house[e] is made for Duke Albrecht V of Bavaria.

- C.7000 BC. The first board games are developed.

- C.2500 BC. Egyptian tomb paintings show hoops used as toys.

- 400 BC. Archytas builds a mechanical bird, one of the earliest powered toys.

- 300–200 BC. The remains of the oldest stuffed toy survive from this period from Ancient Rome.

7000 BC

- C.1000 BC. The Chinese fly kites for fun.

- 200 BC. Greek mathematician Archimedes develops *loculus*, one of the earliest puzzles.

- C.AD 1000. The two-coloured chess board is introduced.

- C.1760. John Spilsbury crea[tes] jigsaws out of maps which boosts the popularity of these puzzles.

- C.3000 BC. Backgammon is developed.

- C.3000 BC. The oldest dolls from Ancient Egypt date from this period.

- AD 950. The earliest reference to a card game from Ancient China.

- c. 1880. Margarete Steiff starts company making stuffed felt toys.

- 1893. Fully rounded toy figures are introduced.

- 1897. Plasticine is invented.

- 1909. The card game gin rummy is played for the first time.

- 1933. Monopoly is developed.

- 1958. Ole Kirk Christiansen invents LEGO.

- 1959. The first Barbie dolls are made.

- 1962. Spacewar! is developed, one of the first computer games.

- 1989. Game Boy is released.

- 2000. Playstation 2 is released.

TODAY

- 1913 The first crossword appears in a newspaper.

- 1948. Fred Morrison produces plastic discs called Frisbees.

- 1983–1987. More than 40 million Care Bears are sold.

- 1902. Theodore Roosevelt refuses to shoot a bear cub, an event that leads to the creation of teddy bears.

- 1980s. Cabbage Patch Dolls are released.

- 1980. The Rubik's cube is released worldwide, becoming an international bestseller.

- 1979. Trivial Pursuit is introduced.

- 1901. Frank Hornby develops a metal building set called Meccano.

- 1978. Space Invaders is introduced.

- 1835. The designs for the modern standard chess set are created.

- 1964. GI Joe is released in the US, becoming the first doll for boys.

29

Factfile

• The world's smallest teddy bear was made by Utaho Imaoka of Japan. It measured just 9 mm long and all of its body parts moved.

• In contrast, the world's largest stitched teddy bear was a whopping 11.79 m long. It was made by Dana Warren of Edmond, Oklahoma, USA.

• Tony Mattia of the UK has the world's largest collection of Barbie dolls. He has 1125 of them and changes all of their costumes every month.

• In 1999, Matt Babeck of the USA paid $14 000 for an original GI Joe figure, making it the world's most expensive toy soldier.

• The world's most expensive teddy bear was made in 1904 by the Steiff company. In 1994, it sold for £110 000.

• The smallest motorised car ever made measured just 4.785 mm in length. It was powered by a coiled spring that was 1mm across and had a bumper that was 50 microns wide – that's half the width of a human hair! It was made by Nippondenso of Kariya, Japan, and it could travel at 0.018 km/h.

Glossary

Backgammon
A board game for two players. The aim is to move your pieces around a board and remove them from play, using dice to decide the number of moves.

Chess
A game for two players who move different pieces around a board. The aim is to trap the opponent's king. This is called checkmate.

Clockwork
A mechanical device that uses a key to wind up a coiled spring. As the spring unwinds, it drives a motor that can be used to power a clock, watch or toy.

Compressed air
Air that has been squashed, increasing its pressure. When the compressed air is released, it flows rapidly and can be used to power a motor.

Deck
The name given to a set of cards. The modern deck of cards has 52 cards that are divided into four suits.

Modelling clay
A special type of clay that will not dry out and go hard, allowing it to be shaped and moulded over and over again.

Middle East
A region that lies between Asia and Africa and includes countries such as Saudi Arabia, Israel, Syria, Egypt, Iraq and Jordan.

Patent
The official document that states the inventor is the only person who can make, use and sell a device.

Poker
A card game in which two or more players try to collect the highest-ranking hand of cards.

Suit
A deck of cards is divided into four groups that are known as suits. These suits are hearts, spades, clubs and diamonds. The cards number one (known as the ace) to ten, plus the royal cards: jack, queen and king.

Whist
A card game for four people that involves the winner laying the highest card.

Index